G is for Gold Medal

An Olympics Alphabet

Written by Brad Herzog and Illustrated by Doug Bowles

To Kris Stejskal, gold medal teacher at Robert Down Elementary,
who taught my sons for four years in a row—an educational Olympiad.

BRAD

❁

To Bet, Lauren, and Adam, to my talented crew at Sleeping Bear,
and to Mr. Jim Thorpe, who has always been an inspiration to me.

DOUG

Text Copyright © 2011 Brad Herzog
Illustration Copyright © 2011 Doug Bowles

Sleeping Bear Press®
315 E. Eisenhower Parkway, Suite 200
Ann Arbor, MI 48108
www.sleepingbearpress.com

Sleeping Bear Press is an imprint of Gale, a part of Cengage Learning.

10 9 8 7 6 5 4 3 2 1

Printed by China Translation & Printing Services Limited,
Guangdong Province, China. 1st printing. 05/2011

Library of Congress Cataloging-in-Publication Data

Herzog, Brad.
G is for gold medal : an Olympics alphabet / written by Brad Herzog;
illustrated by Doug Bowles.
p. cm.
ISBN 978-1-58536-462-6
1. Olympics—Juvenile literature. 2. Alphabet books. I. Bowles, Doug,
ill. II. Title.
GV721.53.H47 2011
796.48—dc22   2010053707

A a

Ancient Greece and Athens, that's our first letter—A. The Olympics began then and there, long ago and far away.

Ancient Greece was a collection of independent city-states that often met on battlefields. But every four years, they agreed to stop fighting each other for a month. During that time, athletes from those regions traveled to Olympia and competed in the Olympic Games, part of a religious festival honoring Zeus, the king of the gods. The first record of the ancient Olympics dates from 776 BC, and the Games survived for at least one thousand years. When the modern Olympics began again in 1896, it seemed appropriate that the first competition would be held in Athens, Greece.

Boxing, wrestling, horse racing, and chariot racing were among the events that took place at the ancient Olympics. The winners received an olive wreath cut from a sacred tree in Olympia. Women were not allowed to compete (there was a separate women's festival honoring the goddess Hera, wife of Zeus). In fact, for hundreds of years, women were not even allowed to watch the Olympic Games. In most events, the male athletes competed without any clothes on!

A baron is a title of nobility in Europe. Without noble Pierre de Coubertin, there would be no Olympic Games today. He was fascinated by ancient Greece and believed that a modern version of the Olympics would foster peace between nations. Coubertin, who served as president of the International Olympic Committee for 29 years, saw his dream come to life in 1896 in Athens, Greece.

Most of the athletes in the first modern Olympics were Greek. Some were simply tourists who decided to participate! All were men. American triple jumper James Connolly became the first gold medalist. Before him, the last known Olympic champ was a boxer named Barasdates who lived more than 1,500 years earlier.

While there are no international truces called during the Olympic Games (in fact, the Olympics of 1916, 1940, and 1944 were canceled due to world wars), the event promotes harmony between the nations of the world.

B is for a baron,
Pierre de Coubertin from France,
who had the bright idea to give
the Olympics another chance.

Bb

C is for all the countries
that come together to compete,
from Canada to Congo,
in winter cold or summer heat.

There were only about a dozen countries represented in the first modern Olympic Games in 1896. However, the 2008 Summer Olympics in Beijing, China, featured more than 10,000 athletes from more than 200 countries, from Afghanistan to Zimbabwe.

Some countries are so small that they send only a single athlete to compete. However, sometimes very small countries come up very big at the Olympics. At the 1980 Winter Games, siblings Hanni and Andreas Wenzel competed for Lichtenstein, a tiny European country with a population of about 35,000 people. Together, they won two gold medals and two silvers for skiing!

C is also for the city of Chamonix, France, which hosted the first Winter Olympic Games in 1924. The event was originally known as International Winter Sports Week. It wasn't until 1926 that it was officially considered the Olympics.

How do you determine the world's best athlete? The decathlon is a good place to start. It measures an athlete's speed, endurance, strength, and jumping ability. When it first appeared at the 1904 Summer Olympics, the decathlon was known as the "All-Around Championship." It consists of ten different events over only a two-day period. The first day's events are the 100-meter dash, long jump, shot put, high jump, and 400-meter run. On the second day, athletes compete in the 110-meter hurdles, discus throw, pole vault, javelin throw, and 1,500-meter run. Points are given for each event, and the man with the highest point total is declared the decathlon champion.

From 1964 through 1980, women competed in their own combined event contest, the five-event pentathlon. In 1984 that became the heptathlon, which consists of seven events—the 100-meter hurdles, 200-meter dash, 800-meter run, high jump, long jump, shot put, and javelin throw. American Jackie Joyner-Kersee, a two-time gold medalist in the heptathlon, set the world record by totaling 7,291 points at the 1988 Summer Games.

D d

D is for the daring deeds
of a decathlete.
Ten events over two days,
it's quite a daunting feat.

E is for extinct events.
Dozens are no more,
like motorboating, rope climbing,
croquet, and tug-of-war.

Early Olympic Games included some events that seem quite peculiar to us today. At one time or another, competitors could be found climbing ropes, driving motorboats, or participating in a tug-of-war (in which the only equipment needed were two teams and one thick rope). Early swimming events included underwater swimming, a plunge for distance, and even an obstacle race in the water!

Sometimes sports that were removed from the schedule are eventually returned to it. Golf and rugby haven't been in the Olympics since the early twentieth century, but they were approved as events in the 2016 Summer Games. Of course, sometimes sports are better off left extinct. At the 1904 Olympic Games, there was a weight lifting event that was given a pretty unfortunate name. Later discontinued, it was called the all-around dumbbell contest!

The five interlocking rings that are the symbol of the Olympic Games and make up the design of the Olympic flag were conceived by Pierre de Coubertin, founder of the modern Olympics. The rings represent the union of the five parts of the world that send athletes to compete in the event: America (North and South America), Europe, Asia, Africa, and Oceania (Australia, New Zealand, and neighboring islands). The six colors on the flag—a white background and the five rings of blue, yellow, black, green, and red—are said to be those that appear on all of the national flags of the world. During the opening ceremony, the Olympic flag is carried into the stadium and then raised on a flagpole in the arena. At the closing ceremony, the mayor of the city passes the flag to the mayor of the next host city.

F f

Our F is the Olympic flag,
five rings of different hues.
When nations connect peacefully,
no one can really lose.

Gg

The star of the 1912 Olympic Games in Stockholm, Sweden, was Jim Thorpe, a Native American whose Indian name (Wa-Tho-Huck) means "Bright Path." He may have been the greatest all-around athlete in history. Thorpe, who also played pro football and baseball after the Olympics, won both the five-event pentathlon and the ten-event decathlon in 1912. Afterward, the King of Sweden told him, "Sir, you are the greatest athlete in the world." Thorpe replied, "Thanks, King."

Thorpe's satisfaction was short-lived. It was soon discovered that he had earned $25 a week for playing minor league baseball. In those days, athletes who had been professionals of any sort were banned from the Olympic Games, so the International Olympic Committee (IOC) removed his name from the record books and asked him to return his medals. It was another 70 years before the IOC, realizing that the punishment had been too harsh, returned the medals to Thorpe's descendants. Thorpe, who died in 1953, is buried in a town that now calls itself Jim Thorpe, Pennsylvania.

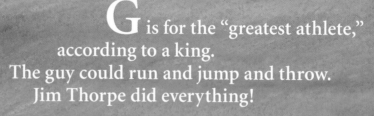

G is for the "greatest athlete,"
according to a king.
The guy could run and jump and throw.
Jim Thorpe did everything!

It isn't often that a kid can transform a sport, but that's what 15-year-old high jumper Dick Fosbury did in 1963. At the time, almost every successful high jumper used a style called the straddle, but it didn't work for Fosbury. So instead of straddling the bar, he jumped shoulders first and upside down, arching his back as he cleared the bar. His competitors thought he looked silly, like a fish flopping into a boat. A photo of him jumping even appeared in newspapers with this caption: WORLD'S LAZIEST HIGH JUMPER.

But it worked. Two years later, after he kept improving his technique, Fosbury finished second in the state high school champion- ship. Within three years, he was the top college high jumper in the nation. But it was at the 1968 Summer Olympics that he became world famous. He achieved a personal best jump of 7 feet, 4¼ inches and won the gold. Within a dozen years, nearly every Olympic finalist was using his jumping style—the Fosbury Flop.

H h

H is for a high jump,
  always a harrowing hop.
"Hah!" they laughed at the inventor
  of the Fosbury Flop.

Ii

A quadruple jump? Impossible!
Inspiring! What a test!
I is for images on the ice
that leave us so impressed.

The winter sport of figure skating—which includes ice dancing, pair skating, and women's and men's singles—actually began as an event in the Summer Olympics! Figure skating is both artistic and athletic. Athletes skate to music, but they also perform incredibly difficult spins, spirals, and jumps. The rare quadruple jump—or "quad"—is perhaps the most difficult, requiring the skater to make at least four revolutions in the air before landing.

Many Olympic events take place on ice. The best male and female hockey players in the world compete, and the world's fastest speed skaters race around a 437-yard oval in individual time trials or, in short track speed skating, around a 122-yard track in tightly-grouped packs. Other icy Olympic sports don't involve skates at all. These include the sledding competitions—bobsled, luge, and skeleton. Curling, which dates back to the sixteenth century, is a bit like shuffleboard on ice. Teams slide a heavy, polished stone toward a target. Two team members with brooms sweep the ice in front of the stone, momentarily melting it. This allows the stone to go farther and stay straighter.

The torch relay is one of the most inspiring elements of any Olympic Games. The Olympic flame is lit in ancient Olympia (Greece) and then carried in specially designed torches across the globe by thousands of different torchbearers in relays. Strangers deliver the flame to strangers as a symbol of international harmony. It is called a torch *relay*, not a torch *run*, because it isn't always on foot. The torch has been carried by swimmers and skiers and cyclists. It has traveled by train, airplane, helicopter, horseback, camel, car, canoe, sailboat, steamboat, snowmobile, and even a reindeer-pulled sled. The torch relay is completed during the opening ceremony, when a national hero lights the Olympic cauldron, which burns throughout the competition.

The first torch relay took place in advance of the 1936 Summer Olympics in Berlin, Germany. The star of those Games was an American track and field athlete Jesse Owens. German leader Adolph Hitler promoted a belief that all races were inferior to the German people. Then Owens, an African-American, showed how absurd that notion was by earning four gold medals!

Jj

J is for a joyous journey
all across the land.
The Olympic flame is carried
and exchanged from hand to hand.

K
k

Most every Olympic sport organizes junior programs to help develop future stars, but Olympic champions have more than just skills. They have determination. In fact, many of them have had tremendous obstacles to overcome as children.

Wilma Rudolph, one of 22 children in her family, lived in poverty, contracted a serious disease called polio, and could barely use her left leg for several years. So what did she do at the 1960 Summer Games? She won three gold medals in track and field!

At the age of two, Scott Hamilton stopped growing properly because his intestines weren't absorbing food. He was quite small, but he discovered that his size didn't prevent him from succeeding in figure skating. So he devoted himself to the sport. Hamilton went on to win four straight U.S. championships and then an Olympic gold medal in 1984.

Before he was even one year old, Shaun White endured two open-heart operations because he was born with a heart defect. "The Flying Tomato" recovered and became a snowboarding legend, winning gold medals in 2006 and 2010.

K is for kids everywhere
who practice hard and dream
of competing for their country
on an Olympic team.

Artistic gymnastics events have introduced some of the most famous Olympic athletes in history. Female Olympic gymnasts compete in four events—vault, uneven bars, balance beam, and floor exercise. Men compete in six events—vault, floor, pommel horse, rings, horizontal bar, and parallel bars. Medals are awarded for total team scores, for each apparatus (piece of equipment), and for the top gymnasts in the all-around competition.

Two tiny American gymnasts earned lasting fame with clutch vault performances despite enormous pressure. In 1984, Mary Lou Retton scored a perfect 10 to become the first American woman to win the all-around title. Twelve years later, Kerri Strug completed her second vault attempt despite having severely injured her ankle on the first attempt. She landed in great pain, but raised her arms in triumph. The Americans won the gold!

There are two other forms of gymnastics at the Olympic Games. In rhythmic gymnastics, women perform balletic movements to music while handling items like clubs, hoops, and ribbons. In trampolining, gymnasts perform acrobatics while bouncing on a trampoline.

L l

A long run starts letter L,
   then a launch, a leap, a landing.
A little gymnast with a large heart.
   A gold medal! Outstanding!

A medal, that's our letter M.
You won! They're cheering loud!
Stand for your national anthem.
You made your country proud.

M
m

At the first modern Olympics, only silver medals (for first place) and copper medals (for second place) were awarded. But ever since, Olympians have received gold for first place, silver for second, and bronze for third. After the event, the top three athletes watch as the flags representing their countries are raised high, and the gold medalist's national anthem is played.

Swimmer Michael Phelps won an amazing 14 Olympic gold medals in 2004 and 2008, giving him four more than any athlete in history. Other gold-collecting Americans include sprinter and long jumper Carl Lewis, who won nine golds in four Olympic Games, and five-time champion speed skaters Eric Heiden and Bonnie Blair.

In 1936, two Japanese pole vaulters tied for second place and were asked to vault against each other to see who would finish ahead. But the friends refused, so one was given the silver, while the other received the bronze. When they returned to Japan, they had a jeweler cut each medal in half and then fuse the different halves together. Each man's medal became a silver-bronze.

With the exception of tennis, table tennis, badminton, and two-person beach volleyball, the net games at the Olympics are team sports. Sometimes the athletes are asked to put a ball through a net, as in basketball. Sometimes they must maneuver a ball over a net, as in indoor volleyball. And sometimes they must hit or kick or throw a ball into a net at the back of a goal, as in field hockey, soccer, team handball, and water polo.

N is also for nicknames. American sprinter Archie Hahn was called the Milwaukee Meteor. Canadian high jumper Ethel Catherwood was the Saskatoon Lily. Runner Paavo Nurmi, a nine-time gold medalist from Finland, was known as the Phantom Finn. But probably the best nickname in Olympic history belonged to 17-year-old Mexican swimmer Felipe Muñoz, who won a gold medal in 1968. Felipe's father was from the town of Aguascalientes, which means "hot waters" in Spanish. Felipe's mother was from Rio Frio, which means "cold river." So Felipe became known as Tibio, which means "lukewarm."

Soccer, volleyball, water polo,
    they all require a net.
        Basketball, badminton, tennis, too.
So that's **N** in our alphabet.

O is the opening ceremony,
an orchestrated celebration
of the history and culture
found in the host nation.

The opening ceremony in the Olympic stadium has become a spectacle that launches the Olympic Games. **O** is also for an opportunity—a chance for the nation hosting the event to put on an extravagant and artistic show honoring both its civilization and the Olympic movement. The 2008 opening ceremony in Beijing, China, featured (among other things) nearly 15,000 performers, exactly 2,008 drummers with glowing drumsticks, the five Olympic rings being lifted by flying acrobats, a 16-ton globe rising from the ground, martial arts dancers, singers, a light show, and a massive fireworks display.

The Parade of Nations is always a centerpiece of the ceremony. Athletes from each country proudly march into the stadium, following one of their own who has been chosen as the flag bearer. The athletes representing Greece enter the stadium first, in honor of the origins of the Olympics. The remaining countries follow in alphabetical order according to the language of the host country, whose athletes are always the last to arrive.

The Paralympic Games bring together physically and mentally disabled athletes in the same host city as the Olympic Games, just a few weeks later. At the 2008 Summer Paralympics, nearly 4,200 athletes traveled to Beijing, China, from 148 countries and competed in 20 different events. The athletes are amazing, whether they are blind cyclists who race on tandem cycles, long jumpers who compete with prostheses (artificial limbs), or marathoners who compete in specialized wheelchairs and reach speeds of more than 35 miles per hour.

The Paralympics are sometimes confused with the Special Olympics. But while Paralympians are world-class athletes, anybody with intellectual disabilities may compete in the Special Olympics. Since its start in 1968, it has become a global movement involving nearly three million athletes from more than 180 countries, as well as World Winter Games and World Summer Games that are held every four years. The true value of the Special Olympics is not in finding a winner, but in allowing these special athletes to find acceptance, friendship, and belief in themselves.

Paralympic athletes,
that's our letter P.
Proud disabled people show
how skillful they can be.

P p

Q is for quadrennial.
Every four years we see
a new host city showing off
its hospitality.

Quadrennial means "happening once every four years." Except for cancellation due to world wars (and except for a special 10th anniversary event in 1906), the Summer Games have taken place every four years since 1896. For a long time, the Winter Olympics were held in the same years as the summer event, but they now take place in alternating even-numbered years.

When it comes time for the International Olympic Committee to select a host for the Games, many cities hope to be chosen because it is an opportunity to exhibit their culture and achievements to the world. When Rio de Janeiro (Brazil) was picked to host the 2016 Summer Games, it was the first South American city so honored. Africa is the only remaining continent, besides Antarctica, that hasn't hosted the Olympics.

The Summer Olympics often take place in major cities such as Montreal (Canada) and Moscow (Russia). But the Winter Games are often held in smaller mountain cities surrounded by natural wonders—places like Lillehammer in Norway and Lake Placid in the Adirondack Mountains of New York.

Run a relay. Row a boat.
Ride a bike. Maintain your pace.
R Paddle through river rapids.
is for a race.

Many Olympic sports are simply all about who can get there first, whether the competitors are swimming in a pool, rowing across a lake, kayaking atop a river, sailing on the ocean, or cycling along a road. One event, the Olympic triathlon, combines a few of these challenges. Athletes must swim 1,500 meters, then bike 40 kilometers, and finally run 10 kilometers.

For at least the first five decades of the ancient Olympic Games, the only event that took place was a short footrace. Today, Olympic spectators can enjoy footraces of all sorts, from the 110-meter hurdles to the 3,000-meter steeplechase (in which athletes must leap over barriers and water jumps) to the 50,000-meter walk. There was no such thing as a "marathon" race until the first modern Olympics in 1896. The 26-mile race (385 yards were added to it in 1908) was the centerpiece of those first Games. However, these days the 100-meter dash is always one of the most exciting races because the winner is given the unofficial title of World's Fastest Human.

Skiing is an electrifying Winter Olympic sport. Downhill skiers reach speeds of nearly 90 miles per hour, and ski jumpers soar through the air for nearly 300 feet. The traditional categories of ski competition at the Winter Games are alpine skiing and Nordic skiing. Alpine events are the familiar downhill and slalom events (skiing between a series of poles). Nordic skiing events are cross-country skiing, ski jumping, and a combination of the two called Nordic combined.

Freestyle skiing, a more recent addition to the Games, includes events such as mogul skiing, aerials, and ski cross. Mogul skiers execute tricks while skiing over a series of snow mounds. Aerialists ski off jumps and perform flips and twists in midair before landing.

Skis aren't the only way someone can get down a snow-covered hill. Snowboarding has been an Olympic sport since 1998, combining elements of skiing and skateboarding. There are half-pipe, giant slalom, and snowboard cross events.

S

S

S is for speedy skiers
schussing through the snow.
Watch them slalom down the slope.
Look how fast they go!

T t

Take aim. It's time to talk about talented athletes who try to hit the target—that's our T. Perfect shot! Bull's-eye!

Target events have been part of the Olympics since the first modern Games in 1896. In Olympic archery, archers use something called a recurve bow, which can propel arrows at more than 150 miles per hour. Each archer stands 70 meters from a target divided into ten rings. The innermost (and smallest) ring is worth ten points, and each ring further from the center is worth one less point. There are also more than a dozen shooting events in which competitors aim at stationary targets with pistols or rifles and at moving clay targets with shotguns. At the 1980 Summer Olympics, Luciano Giovannetti of Italy finished in first place in trap shooting. He responded by tossing his cap into the air and shooting a hole through it!

"Do you believe in miracles?" sportscaster Al Michaels asked in the closing seconds of a hockey game between the United States and the Soviet Union. At the 1980 Winter Games in Lake Placid, New York, the Americans, a group of college-aged amateurs, were not expected to win a hockey medal. By comparison, the Soviets were so good that they had beaten a group of National Hockey League (NHL) all-stars 6-0 a year earlier. But the Americans won 4-3 and eventually earned the gold medal—the ultimate sports upset!

The hockey team's triumph at the 1980 Winter Games is known as the "Miracle on Ice." But 20 years later, the Summer Games had its "Miracle on the Mat." In Sydney, Australia, Rulon Gardner, the youngest of nine children raised on a dairy farm in Wyoming, defeated Russian Aleksandr Karelin to win the Greco-Roman wrestling gold medal. Karelin, a three-time Olympic gold medalist, hadn't been defeated in 13 years! He hadn't even given up a point in six years!

U u

U is for an underdog,
so unbelievably bold,
and an unexpected upset
to win Olympic gold.

Boxers punching, fencers lunging,
horses jumping, too.
V is for the variety of
Olympic sports to view.

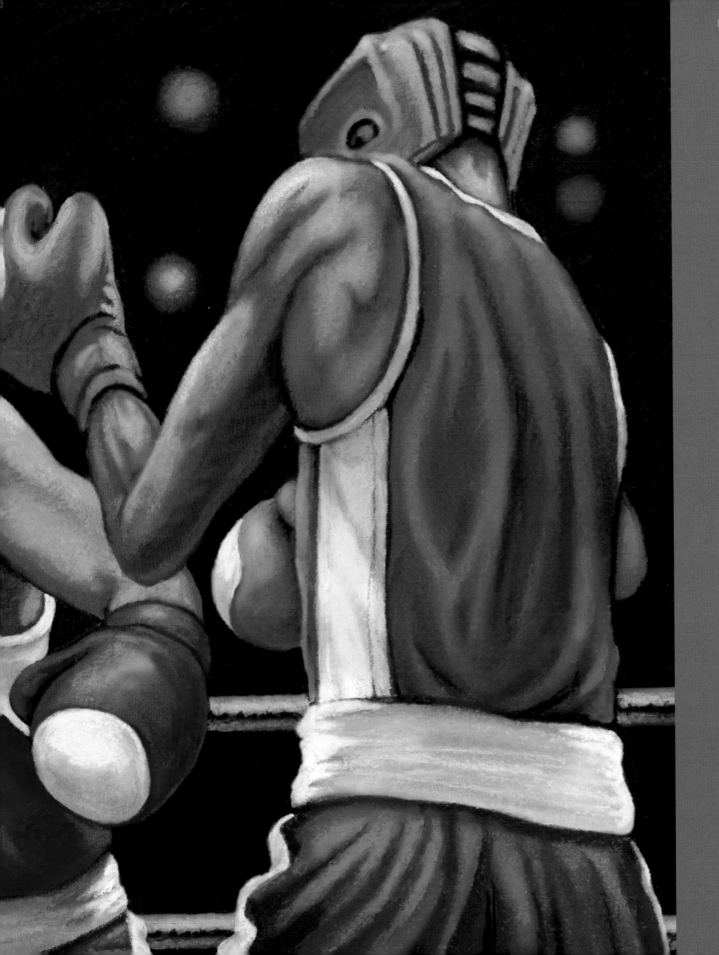

V v

The Olympics allow us to appreciate a variety of people, places, and athletic skills. Athletes in the Summer Games compete in more than 300 team and individual events within more than two dozen sports ranging from the martial art of tae kwon do to table tennis. Perhaps no event better displays athletic variety than the modern pentathlon, which consists of fencing, pistol shooting, a 200-meter freestyle swim, a 3-kilometer cross-country run, and an equestrian (horse-riding) event. A unique winter sport, the biathlon, combines cross-country skiing and rifle shooting.

Female athletes were not allowed to compete in the first modern Olympics, but today women earn medals in everything from weight lifting and wrestling to judo and mountain biking. Women's boxing was added as an Olympic sport for the 2012 Summer Games. Two events, synchronized swimming and rhythmic gymnastics, have featured only female athletes. In most sports, men and women compete separately. However, in Olympic equestrian and sailing events, women and men compete against each other.

V is also for the Olympic Village, where most athletes, coaches, trainers, and officials live during the Olympic Games.

Every event at the Winter Olympics is contested on either snow or ice, but water is the setting for many Summer Olympics sports. Often, this means world-class athletes speeding over rivers, lakes, or bays on watercrafts, whether the sport is sailing, rowing, canoeing (with single-blade paddles), or kayaking (with double-blade paddles).

In the sport of swimming, there are nearly three dozen different events for men and women, from 50-meter races that last less than half a minute to 10-kilometer marathons in which athletes swim for nearly two hours. At the 1952 Summer Games, after swimmer Jean Boiteux of France won the 400-meter freestyle event, his father jumped right into the pool with all of his clothes on and hugged his son.

There are also many other Olympic sports at the swimming pool. Water polo players tread water and wait for an opportune time to fire the ball into a net. Divers leap off platforms 10 meters high and perform back somersaults and twists. Synchronized swimmers perform water ballets.

Gather 'round the pool.
Not too close or you'll get wet!
The wondrous world of water sports
is W in our alphabet.

X x

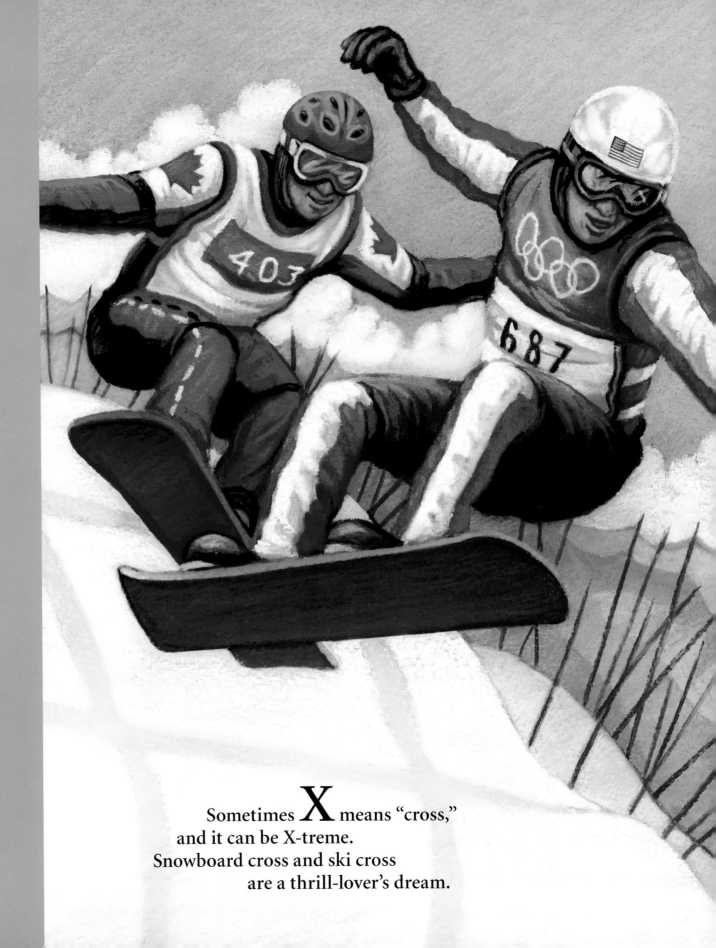

Ski cross (sometimes known as skier-X) and snowboard cross (often called boarder-cross or snowboarder-X) are two recent additions to the Winter Olympic schedule. The sports were invented in the late 1980s and early 1990s as a way to make downhill racing more exciting for spectators. They owe much of their popularity to being part of the X Games, the annual action sports extravaganza patterned after the Olympic Games.

In both sports, participants compete against each other, not against the clock, as they race down an inclined course in groups of four. The course is filled with jumps, drops, and turns. Intentional physical contact is not allowed, but often the racers get their equipment tangled, so spectacular falls are not uncommon. The first two racers to cross the finish line (out of each foursome) move on to the next round of competition until the fastest four compete in the finals.

Sometimes X means "cross,"
and it can be X-treme.
Snowboard cross and ski cross
are a thrill-lover's dream.

Yy

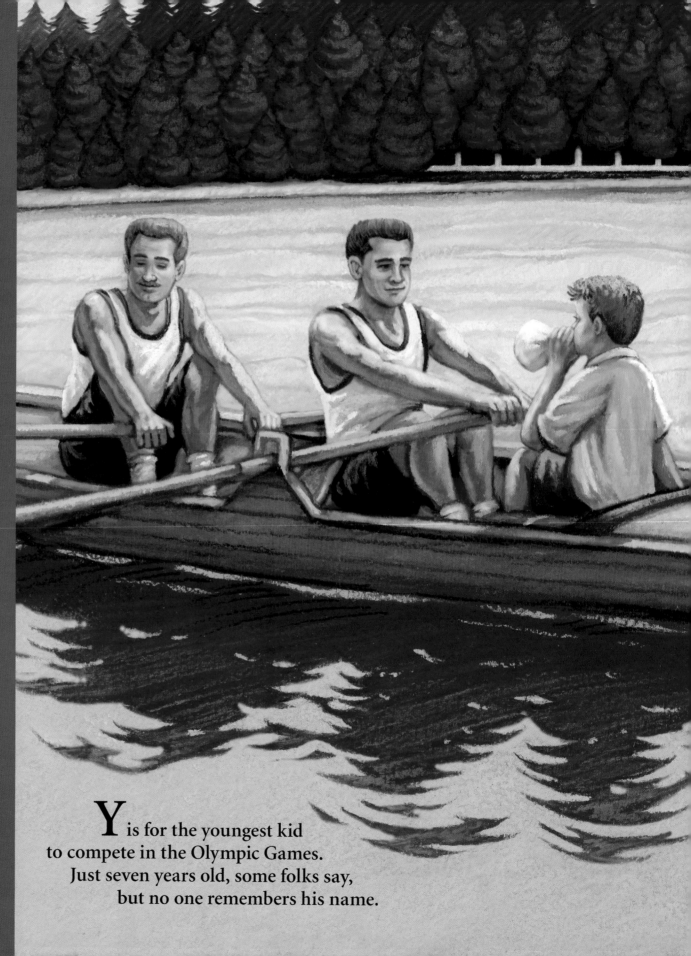

Something remarkable happened at the 1900 Summer Olympics in Paris, France. It occurred during a rowing event called coxed pairs, which features boats with two rowers and one coxswain (a lightweight person who sits in the boat and directs the rowers). Before the finals of the event, the team from Holland decided that the coxswain they normally used was too heavy. So the rowers replaced him with a young French boy that they plucked from the crowd (which wouldn't be allowed these days). The boy, whose name has been lost to history, may have been as young as seven years old! He and his new teammates won the gold medal!

The oldest man to receive an Olympic medal was awarded it 50 years after he competed! Ski jumper Anders Haugen, an American born in Norway, believed he had finished fourth way back in 1924. But five decades later, it was discovered that a scoring error had been made, and Haugen had really finished third. He received his bronze medal in a special ceremony. By then, he was 83 years old!

Y is for the youngest kid
to compete in the Olympic Games.
Just seven years old, some folks say,
but no one remembers his name.

The Olympic motto is Citius, Altius, Fortius, which is Latin for "Swifter, Higher, Stronger." Whether the athlete is a hockey player rushing toward a loose puck, a diver springing into the air far above a pool, or a decathlete throwing a discus with every ounce of effort, each is constantly trying to improve and reach his or her ultimate potential.

At the opening ceremony of every Olympic Games, a single athlete recites an oath: "In the name of all the competitors, I promise that we shall take part in these Olympic Games, respecting and abiding by the rules which govern them, in the true spirit of sportsmanship, for the glory of our sport, and the honor of our teams."

In the opening ceremony, the athletes walk in with their teammates and stand as separate nations. However, during the closing ceremony many athletes mingle with their competitors from other countries. The Olympics have become a global spectacle promoting not only personal achievement, but also peace and understanding.

Z z

The ancient Olympics honored Zeus, our Z, but those games are no longer. Today's athletes honor their sports by going "Swifter, Higher, Stronger."

Summer Olympic Sites	Winter Olympic Sites
1896 - Athens, Greece	1924 - Chamonix, France
1900 - Paris, France	1928 - St. Moritz, Switzerland
1904 - St. Louis, United States	1932 - Lake Placid, United States
1908 - London, United Kingdom	1936 - Garmisch-Partenkirchen, Germany
1912 - Stockholm, Sweden	1948 - St. Moritz, Switzerland
1920 - Antwerp, Belgium	1952 - Oslo, Norway
1924 - Paris, France	1956 - Cortina d'Ampezzo, Italy
1928 - Amsterdam, Netherlands	1960 - Squaw Valley, California, United States
1932 - Los Angeles, United States	1964 - Innsbruck, Austria
1936 - Berlin, Germany	1968 - Grenoble, France
1948 - London, United Kingdom	1972 - Sapporo, Japan
1952 - Helsinki, Finland	1976 - Innsbruck, Austria
1956 - Melbourne, Australia	1980 - Lake Placid, United States
1960 - Rome, Italy	1984 - Sarajevo, Yugoslavia (now Bosnia and Herzegovina)
1964 - Tokyo, Japan	1988 - Calgary, Canada
1968 - Mexico City, Mexico	1992 - Albertville, France
1972 - Munich, West Germany (now Germany)	1994 - Lillehammer, Norway
1976 - Montreal, Canada	1998 - Nagano, Japan
1980 - Moscow, U.S.S.R. (now Russia)	2002 - Salt Lake City, United States
1984 - Los Angeles, United States	2006 - Torino (Turin), Italy
1988 - Seoul, South Korea	2010 - Vancouver, Canada
1992 - Barcelona, Spain	2014 - Sochi, Russia
1996 - Atlanta, United States	
2000 - Sydney, Australia	
2004 - Athens, Greece	
2008 - Beijing, China	
2012 - London, United Kingdom	
2016 - Rio de Janeiro, Brazil	

Due to World War I, Summer Olympic Games were not held in 1916.
Due to World War II, both the Summer Games and Winter Games were cancelled in 1940 and 1944.